USBORNE FIRST READING

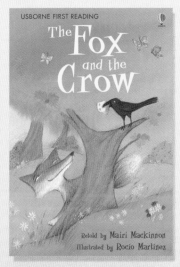

USBORNE FIRST READING

The Fox and the Crow

Retold by Mairi Mackinnon
Illustrated by Rocio Martinez

USBORNE FIRST READING

The Three Wishes

Retold by Lesley Sims
Illustrated by Elisa Squillace

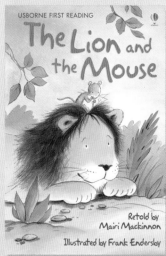

USBORNE FIRST READING

The Lion and the Mouse

Retold by Mairi Mackinnon
Illustrated by Frank Endersby

USBORNE FIRST READING

The Sun and the Wind

Retold by Mairi Mackinnon
Illustrated by Francesca di Chiara

Under the Ground

Anna Milbourne

Illustrated by
Serena Riglietti

Reading consultant: Alison Kelly
Roehampton University

This story is about

Lenny

and Lola

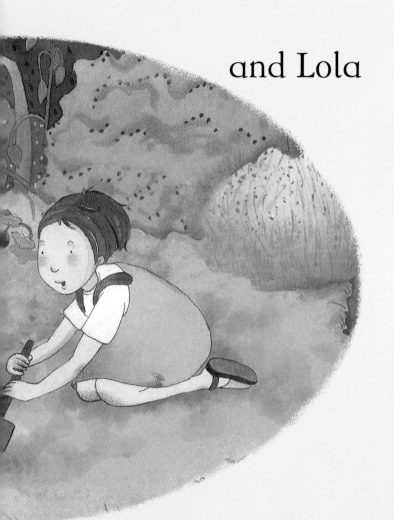

and what they find
under the ground.

"What's under the ground?" asks Lenny.

First they find plant roots

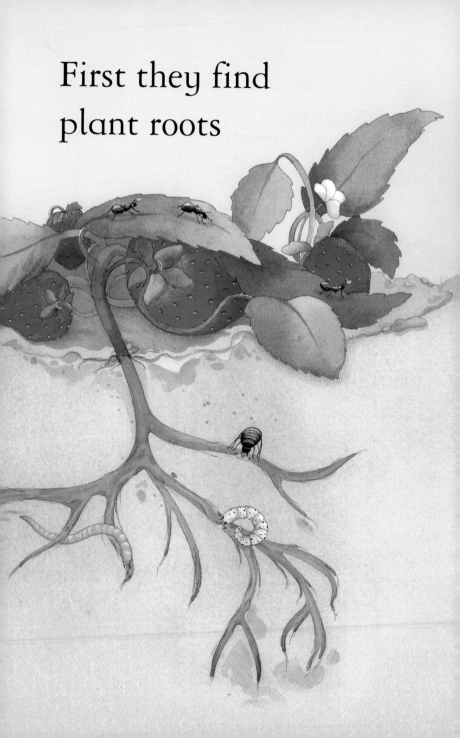

and an ants'
nest.

A mole is eating
a worm.

slurp slurp

8

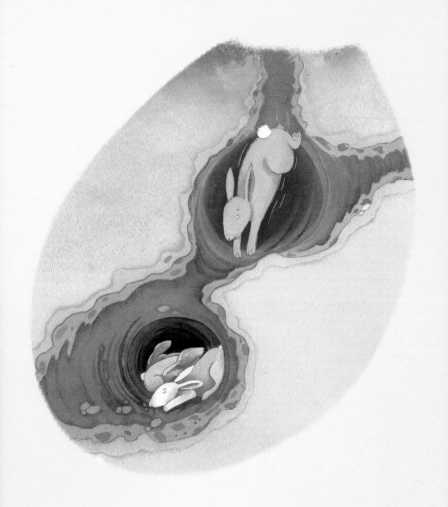

Rabbits snuggle
in their burrow.

Lenny and Lola dig
deep under their
house.

There are lots
of pipes.

There's a rumble
in the tunnels.

12

Trains zoom by.

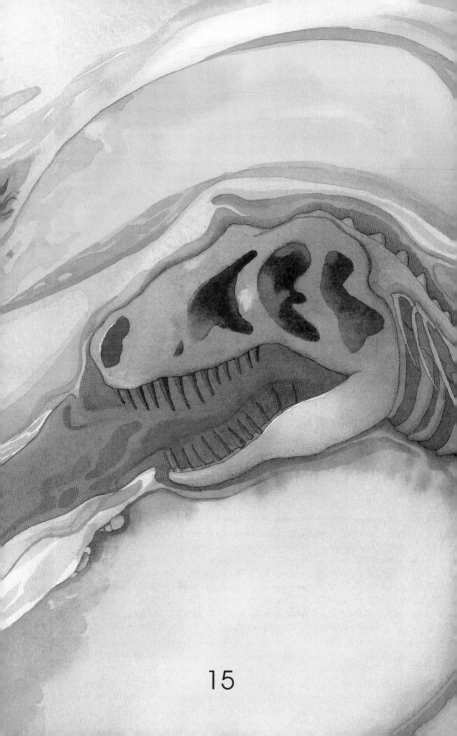

They discover
a damp, dark cave.

Now they are
in a mine.

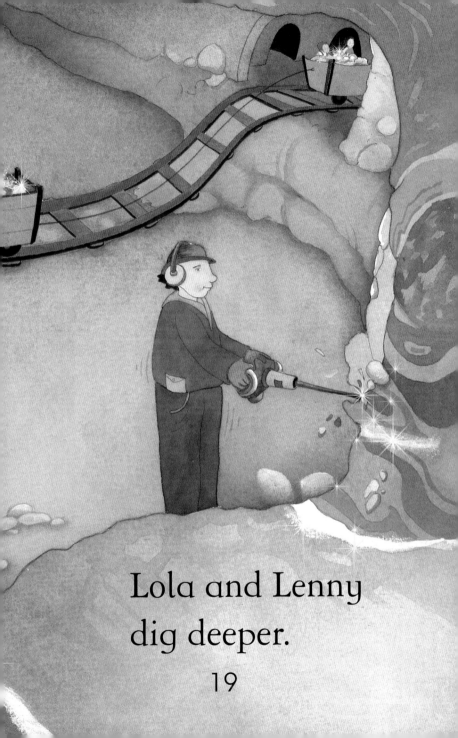

Lola and Lenny
dig deeper.

19

They dig...

and dig, until...

...they pop out on the
other side of the world!

About the Earth

The Earth is a big, round
ball. Here it is cut in half
so you can see inside:

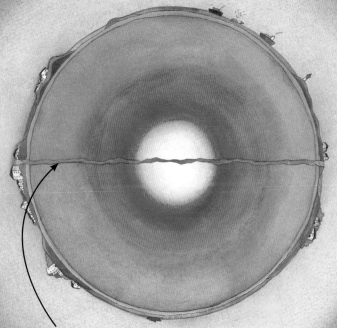

This is where Lenny
and Lola dug.

PUZZLES

Puzzle 1

Can you match the animals to their homes?

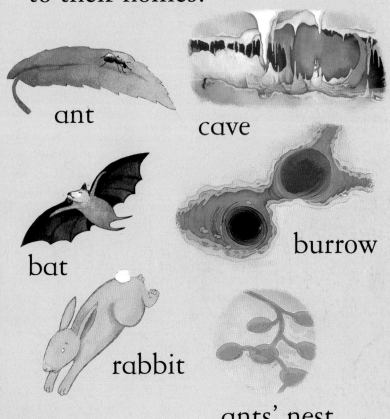

ant

cave

bat

burrow

rabbit

ants' nest

Puzzle 2

Can you choose the right speech bubble for each picture?

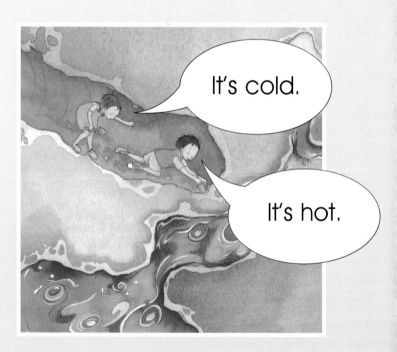

Puzzle 3

Can you spot the differences
between these two pictures?

There are six to find.

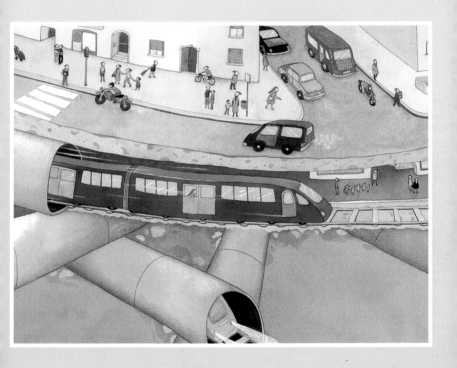

Answers to puzzles

Puzzle 1

ant

ants' nest

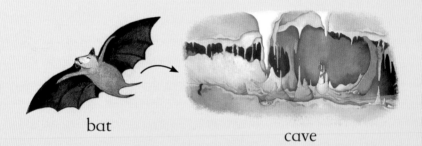
bat

cave

rabbit

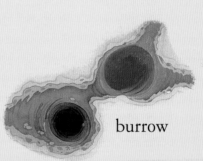
burrow

Puzzle 2

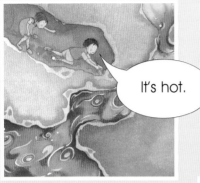

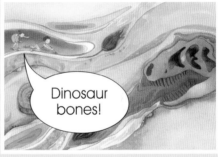

Puzzle 3

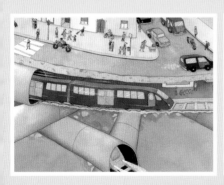

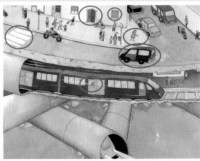

Consultants: Professor Dorrik A. V. Stow
and Drs. Margaret and John Rostron
Design: Emily Bornoff
Series editor: Lesley Sims
Digital manipulation: Nick Wakeford

This edition first published in 2011 by Usborne Publishing Ltd.,
Usborne House, 83-85 Saffron Hill, London EC1N 8RT, England.
www.usborne.com
Copyright © 2011, 2006 Usborne Publishing Ltd.

USBORNE FIRST READING
Level Two

USBORNE FIRST READING

Stone Soup

Retold by Lesley Sims
Illustrated by Georgien Overwater

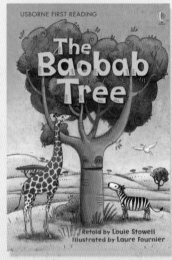

USBORNE FIRST READING

The Baobab Tree

Retold by Louie Stowell
Illustrated by Laure Fournier

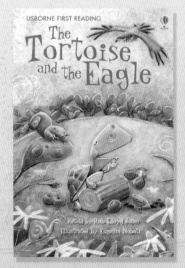

USBORNE FIRST READING

The Tortoise and the Eagle

Retold by Rob Lloyd Jones
Illustrated by Eugenia Nobati

USBORNE FIRST READING

The Genie in the Bottle

Retold by Rosie Dickins
Illustrated by Sara Rojo